Better Homes and Gardens.

Beef & Pork

Easy Everyday Recipe Library

BETTER HOMES AND GARDENS® BOOKS
Des Moines, Iowa

EASY EVERYDAY RECIPE LIBRARY
Better Homes and Gardens® Books, An imprint of Meredith® Books
Published for Creative World Enterprises LP, West Chester, Pennsylvania
www.creativeworldcooking.com

Beef & Pork
Project Editors: Spectrum Communication Services, Inc.
Project Designers: Seif Visual Communications
Copy Chief: Catherine Hamrick
Copy and Production Editor: Terri Fredrickson
Contributing Proofreaders: Kathy Eastman, Susan J. Kling
Electronic Production Coordinator: Paula Forest
Editorial and Design Assistants: Judy Bailey, Mary Lee Gavin, Karen Schirm
Test Kitchen Director: Lynn Blanchard
Production Director: Douglas M. Johnston
Production Managers: Pam Kvitne, Marjorie J. Schenkelberg

Meredith® Books
Editor in Chief: James D. Blume
Design Director: Matt Strelecki
Managing Editor: Gregory H. Kayko

Director, Sales & Marketing, Retail: Michael A. Peterson
Director, Sales & Marketing, Special Markets: Rita McMullen
Director, Sales & Marketing, Home & Garden Center Channel: Ray Wolf
Director, Operations: George A. Susral

Vice President, General Manager: Jamie L. Martin

Better Homes and Gardens® Magazine
Editor in Chief: Jean LemMon
Executive Food Editor: Nancy Byal

Meredith Publishing Group
President, Publishing Group: Christopher M. Little
Vice President, Consumer Marketing & Development: Hal Oringer

Meredith Corporation
Chairman and Chief Executive Officer: William T. Kerr

Chairman of the Executive Committee: E. T. Meredith III

Creative World Enterprises LP
Publisher: Richard J. Petrone
Design Consultants to Creative World Enterprises: Coastline Studios, Orlando, Florida

All of us at Better Homes and Gardens® Books are dedicated to providing you with the information and ideas you need to create delicious foods. We welcome your comments and suggestions. Write to us at: Better Homes and Gardens Books, Cookbook Editorial Department, 1716 Locust St., Des Moines, Iowa 50309-3023.

Our seal assures you that every recipe in *Beef & Pork* has been tested in the Better Homes and Gardens® Test Kitchen. This means that each recipe is practical and reliable, and meets our high standards of taste appeal. We guarantee your satisfaction with this book for as long as you own it.

Cover photo: Tenderloin Steaks with Arugula-Cornichon Relish (see recipe, page 10)

Whether you're planning a weeknight meal for your family or a special dinner for friends, beef and pork dishes are always a delicious choice. You can choose from a number of different cooking methods, including broiling, frying, roasting, grilling, stewing, or even baking. And today's leaner cuts have less fat and supply protein, vitamins, and iron to your diet.

The creative recipes in this book will help you rediscover favorite ways of serving these flavorful meats. Try a few of these exciting beef and pork dishes—they're sure to delight everyone at your dinner table.

CONTENTS

Grilled Rump Roast with Curried Mustard

A mixture of mustard, honey, curry powder, and chives makes a glistening glaze for the roast. Then stir the remaining mustard mixture into sour cream for a refreshing sauce.

1 3-pound boneless beef round
    rump roast
2 tablespoons Dijon-style mustard
1 tablespoon honey
1 teaspoon curry powder
1 teaspoon snipped fresh chives
½ cup dairy sour cream
   Snipped fresh chives (optional)

Trim fat from meat. Stir together mustard, honey, curry powder, and 1 teaspoon chives. Measure about 1 tablespoon of the mustard mixture; brush over meat. Insert a meat thermometer into the center of the meat.

For sauce, in a small bowl combine the remaining mustard mixture and sour cream. Cover and chill till serving time.

In a covered grill arrange medium coals around a drip pan. Test for medium-low heat above the pan. Place meat on grill rack over drip pan. Cover and grill to desired doneness. [Allow 1¼ to 1¾ hours for medium rare (140°) or 1¾ to 2¼ hours for medium (155°).]

Remove meat from grill and cover with foil. Let stand for 15 minutes before slicing. (The meat's temperature will rise 5° during standing.)

Serve the meat with sauce and, if desired, additional snipped chives. Makes 12 servings.

Nutrition information per serving: 202 calories, 26 g protein, 2 g carbohydrate, 9 g fat (4 g saturated), 81 mg cholesterol, 108 mg sodium.

Rib Eyes with Grilled Garlic

The garlic cloves mellow in flavor as they cook, making a delicious sauce for most any grilled meat or poultry. And for an appetizer, spread the softened cloves over toasted slices of French bread.

2   12-ounce boneless beef rib eye
       steaks, cut 1 inch thick
1   whole head of garlic
2   tablespoons olive oil or cooking oil
1   tablespoon snipped fresh basil or
       ½ teaspoon dried basil, crushed
1   tablespoon snipped fresh rosemary
       or ½ teaspoon dried rosemary,
       crushed

Trim fat from steaks. Set aside. Fold a 24x18-inch piece of heavy foil in half to make an 18x12-inch rectangle. Remove the papery outer layers from garlic head. Cut off and discard about ½ inch from top of garlic head to expose the garlic cloves.

Place garlic head in center of foil. Bring the foil up around the garlic on all sides, forming a cup. Drizzle garlic with oil; sprinkle with basil and rosemary. Twist the ends of the foil together to completely enclose the garlic in the foil.

Grill the steaks and packet of garlic on an uncovered grill directly over medium coals till steaks are desired doneness, turning once. (Allow 8 to 12 minutes for medium rare or 12 to 15 minutes for medium.)

Transfer steaks to a platter. Open packet of garlic. Drizzle oil from packet over steaks. Lift the softened cloves of garlic from head; spread garlic over steaks. If desired, sprinkle with salt and pepper. Cut steaks into serving-size pieces. Makes 4 servings.

Nutrition information per serving: 366 calories, 34 g protein, 2 g carbohydrate, 24 g fat (8 g saturated), 100 mg cholesterol, 226 mg sodium.

Grilled Southwest Steak

Balance the spiciness by serving a cooling fruit salsa with the grilled steak. Simply toss together 1 cup chopped fresh peaches or apricots, ¼ cup chopped green or red sweet pepper, 2 tablespoons sliced green onion, 1 tablespoon honey, and 1 tablespoon lime juice.

1	pound beef round steak, cut 1 inch thick
⅓	cup cooking oil
⅓	cup lime juice
3	jalapeño peppers, chopped
3	shallots, chopped
2	tablespoons snipped cilantro
2	cloves garlic, minced
¼	teaspoon salt

Trim fat from steak. Place steak in a plastic bag and set the bag into a shallow dish. For marinade, in a small bowl stir together oil, lime juice, jalapeño peppers, shallots, cilantro, garlic, and salt. Pour over steak; seal bag. Marinate in the refrigerator for 6 hours or overnight, turning bag occasionally.

Drain steak, reserving marinade. Grill steak on an uncovered grill directly over medium coals to desired doneness, turning once. (Allow 14 to 16 minutes for medium rare or 18 to 20 minutes for medium.) Brush occasionally with marinade up to the last 5 minutes of grilling. Makes 4 servings.

Nutrition information per serving: 229 calories, 27 g protein, 1 g carbohydrate, 12 g fat (3 g saturated), 72 mg cholesterol, 186 mg sodium.

Tenderloin Steaks with Arugula-Cornichon Relish

Most people love a good steak, but it's better yet with this caper and fresh-herb relish. Peppery arugula, a built-in salad, offers a pleasant bite. (Also pictured on the cover.)

4 beef tenderloin steaks (or 2 halved boneless rib eye steaks), cut 1 inch thick (about 1 pound total)
1 tablespoon cracked pepper
½ teaspoon salt
3 tablespoons olive oil
⅓ cup snipped Italian flat-leaf parsley
3 tablespoons finely chopped cornichons or sweet pickles
2 tablespoons capers, drained and coarsely chopped
1 medium green onion, chopped
1 tablespoon balsamic vinegar
3 cups torn arugula and/or torn mixed greens

Trim fat from steaks. Rub both sides of steaks with pepper and salt. In a large skillet heat 1 tablespoon of the olive oil over medium heat. Add the steaks and cook to desired doneness, turning once. (Allow 8 to 11 minutes for medium rare or 12 to 14 minutes for medium).

Meanwhile, for relish, in a small mixing bowl combine the remaining olive oil, Italian parsley, cornichons or sweet pickles, capers, green onion, and balsamic vinegar. Set aside.

To serve, transfer steaks to a cutting board. Cut into thin slices. Arrange the arugula or mixed greens on dinner plates. Top with the steak slices, then spoon the relish over steak and arugula. Makes 4 servings.

Nutrition information per serving: 273 calories, 23 g protein, 6 g carbohydrate, 18 g fat (4 g saturated), 64 mg cholesterol, 460 mg sodium.

All About Arugula

Arugula, sometimes called rocket, is a peppery, pungent salad green that adds a spicy flavor to dishes. Select arugula with fresh, small, rich green leaves. Avoid yellowed or wilted leaves. When you bring arugula home, refrigerate it in a plastic bag for up to 2 days. To use it, gently wash the leaves by immersing them in cold water until there is no trace of grit and sand. Pat the leaves dry with paper towels.

Garlic Steaks with Nectarine-Onion Relish

What's better than the smell of steak on the grill in the summertime? The aroma of garlic-studded beef on the grill. Serve this steak with some crusty bread to soak up the delicious juices.

4 boneless beef top loin steaks, cut
   1 inch thick
6 cloves garlic, thinly sliced
2 medium onions, coarsely chopped
1 teaspoon olive oil
2 tablespoons cider vinegar
1 tablespoon honey
1 medium nectarine, chopped
2 teaspoons snipped fresh applemint,
   pineapplemint, or spearmint
   Fresh applemint, pineapplemint,
   or spearmint sprigs (optional)

Trim fat from steaks. With the point of a paring knife, make small slits in steaks. Insert half of the garlic slices into slits. Wrap steaks in plastic wrap; let stand at room temperature up to 20 minutes. (For more intense flavor, chill up to 8 hours.) Sprinkle steaks with salt and pepper.

Meanwhile, for relish, in a large nonstick skillet cook onions and remaining garlic in hot oil over medium heat about 10 minutes or till onions are a deep golden color (but not brown), stirring occasionally. Stir in vinegar and honey. Stir in nectarine and the snipped mint. Heat through.

Grill steaks on an uncovered grill directly over medium coals to desired doneness, turning once. (Allow 8 to 12 minutes for medium rare or 12 to 15 minutes for medium.) Serve the relish with steaks. If desired, garnish with mint sprigs. Makes 4 servings.

Nutrition information per serving: 272 calories, 34 g protein, 13 g carbohydrate, 9 g fat (3 g saturated), 97 mg cholesterol, 108 mg sodium.

Hearty Beef Salad with Horseradish Dressing

In the summertime, grill the sirloin steak for this tasty salad. Place the meat on a rack of an uncovered grill directly over medium coals. Grill for 8 to 12 minutes for medium rare or 12 to 15 minutes for medium.

8	ounces green beans
1½	cups packaged, peeled baby carrots
12	ounces beef sirloin steak, cut 1 inch thick
4	cups torn Boston or Bibb lettuce
1	16-ounce can julienne beets, rinsed and drained
	Horseradish Dressing
	Cracked pepper (optional)

Wash green beans; remove ends and strings. Cut beans in half crosswise. In a covered medium saucepan cook beans in boiling water for 5 minutes. Add baby carrots and cook for 10 to 15 minutes more or till vegetables are tender; drain. Cover and chill for 4 to 24 hours.

Trim fat from meat. Place meat on the unheated rack of a broiler pan. Broil 3 to 4 inches from the heat to desired doneness, turning once. (Allow 10 to 12 minutes for medium rare or 12 to 15 minutes for medium.) Thinly slice across grain into bite-size strips.

Divide torn lettuce among salad plates. Arrange green beans, baby carrots, meat slices, and beets on lettuce. Spoon the Horseradish Dressing over salads. If desired, sprinkle each serving with pepper. Makes 4 servings.

Horseradish Dressing: In a small mixing bowl beat together ½ of a 3-ounce package *cream cheese*, softened, and 2 tablespoons *horseradish sauce*. Stir in enough *milk* (3 to 4 tablespoons) to make of drizzling consistency. Cover and chill till serving time. (Dressing will thicken slightly if made ahead and chilled.)

Nutrition information per serving: 360 calories, 32 g protein, 24 g carbohydrate, 15 g fat (6 g saturated), 94 mg cholesterol, 497 mg sodium.

Flank Steak Salad with Pineapple Salsa

The fresh-tasting fruit salsa that enlivens this warm steak salad starts with green picante sauce. Just add pineapple, sweet pepper, and mandarin oranges—and serve.

2 cups chopped, peeled and cored fresh pineapple
1 11-ounce can mandarin orange sections, drained
½ cup chopped red and/or green sweet pepper
⅓ cup mild green picante sauce or green taco sauce
12 ounces beef flank or boneless sirloin steak, cut ½ inch thick
½ teaspoon Mexican seasoning or chili powder
1 tablespoon olive oil
4 to 6 cups torn mixed greens

For pineapple salsa, in a medium bowl gently stir together pineapple, mandarin oranges, sweet pepper, and picante or taco sauce. Set aside.

Trim fat from meat. Thinly slice across the grain into bite-size strips. Sprinkle with Mexican seasoning or chili powder; toss to coat evenly.

In a large skillet cook and stir half of the seasoned meat in hot oil over medium-high heat for 2 to 3 minutes or to desired doneness. Remove from skillet. Repeat with the remaining meat.

Arrange mixed greens on dinner plates. Top with meat and pineapple salsa. Makes 4 servings.

Nutrition information per serving: 245 calories, 18 g protein, 23 g carbohydrate, 10 g fat (3 g saturated), 40 mg cholesterol, 224 mg sodium.

Preparing Pineapple

To peel and core a pineapple, first slice off the bottom stem end and the green top. Stand the pineapple on one cut end and slice off the skin in wide strips from top to bottom. Remove the eyes by cutting diagonally around the fruit, following the pattern of the eyes and making narrow wedge-shaped grooves. Cut away as little of the fruit as possible. Then slice or chop the fruit away from the core. Discard core.

Spicy Thai Ginger Beef

Thai cooking is strongly influenced by both Chinese and Indian cuisines. In fact, the Thai people migrated from China's Yunnan province in the 13th century.

12 ounces beef top round steak
1 tablespoon fish sauce
1 tablespoon water
1 teaspoon finely shredded lime peel
1 tablespoon lime juice
1 teaspoon sugar
1 tablespoon cooking oil
2 medium zucchini, cut into julienne strips (2 cups)
6 green onions, bias-cut into 1-inch pieces (1 cup)
1 fresh, pickled, or canned jalapeño pepper, seeded and finely chopped
3 cloves garlic, minced
2 teaspoons grated gingerroot
2 cups hot cooked rice sticks or rice
2 tablespoons snipped cilantro

Trim fat from meat. Partially freeze meat. Thinly slice across the grain into bite-size strips. Set aside.

For sauce, in a small bowl stir together fish sauce, water, lime peel, lime juice, and sugar. Set aside.

Add cooking oil to a wok or large skillet. Preheat over medium-high heat (add more oil if necessary during cooking). Stir-fry zucchini in hot oil for 1 to 2 minutes or till crisp-tender. Remove zucchini from wok. Add green onions to wok; stir-fry for 1½ minutes. Remove green onions from wok.

Add jalapeño pepper, garlic and gingerroot to wok. Stir-fry for 15 seconds. Add meat; stir-fry for 2 to 3 minutes or to desired doneness. Return zucchini and green onions to wok.

Add sauce. Cook and stir about 2 minutes more or till heated through. Serve immediately with hot cooked rice sticks or rice. Sprinkle with cilantro. Makes 3 servings.

Nutrition information per serving: 339 calories, 31 g protein, 30 g carbohydrate, 10 g fat (3 g saturated fat), 74 mg cholesterol, 242 mg sodium.

Beef and Vegetables in Oyster Sauce

Oyster sauce, a favorite seasoning in Cantonese dishes, is thick and brown and, as the name implies, made from an extract of oysters. It is available in both bottles and cans and should be refrigerated after opening.

1 pound beef top round steak
¼ cup oyster sauce
1 tablespoon soy sauce
⅛ teaspoon pepper
1 tablespoon cooking oil
3 cloves garlic, minced
1 medium onion, cut into thin wedges
4 cups bok choy, cut into 1-inch pieces
2 cups fresh pea pods, strings removed, or one 6-ounce package frozen pea pods, thawed
2 small tomatoes, cut into thin wedges
2 cups hot cooked rice

Trim fat from meat. Partially freeze meat. Thinly slice across the grain into bite-size strips. Set aside.

For sauce, in a small bowl stir together oyster sauce, soy sauce, and pepper. Set aside.

Add cooking oil to a wok or large skillet. Preheat over medium-high heat (add more oil if necessary during cooking). Stir-fry garlic in hot oil for 15 seconds. Add onion; stir-fry for 2 minutes. Add bok choy and pea pods; stir-fry about 3 minutes or till vegetables are crisp-tender. Remove vegetables from wok.

Add half of the meat to wok. Stir-fry for 2 to 3 minutes or to desired doneness. Remove from wok. Repeat with the remaining meat. Return all of the meat to wok.

Return cooked vegetables to wok. Add tomatoes and sauce. Stir all ingredients together to coat. Cook and stir for 1 to 2 minutes more or till heated through. Serve immediately over hot rice. Makes 4 servings.

Nutrition information per serving: 382 calories, 34 g protein, 39 g carbohydrate, 10 g fat (3 g saturated fat), 77 mg cholesterol, 883 mg sodium.

Orange-Beef Stir-Fry

In this mild version of a classic Szechwan recipe, we've rounded out the dish with the addition of crisp water chestnuts and fresh spinach.

12 ounces beef top round steak
1 teaspoon finely shredded orange peel
½ cup orange juice
1 tablespoon cornstarch
1 tablespoon soy sauce
1 teaspoon sugar
1 teaspoon instant beef bouillon granules
1 tablespoon cooking oil
4 green onions, bias-sliced into 1-inch pieces (⅔ cup)
1 clove garlic, minced
6 cups coarsely shredded spinach (8 ounces)
½ of an 8-ounce can sliced water chestnuts, drained
2 cups hot cooked rice
Slivered orange peel (optional)

Trim fat from meat. Partially freeze meat. Thinly slice across the grain into bite-size strips. Set aside.

For sauce, in a small bowl stir together shredded orange peel, orange juice, cornstarch, soy sauce, sugar, and bouillon granules. Set aside.

Add cooking oil to a wok or large skillet. Preheat over medium-high heat (add more oil if necessary during cooking). Stir-fry green onions and garlic in hot oil for 1 minute. Remove green onion mixture from wok.

Add meat to wok. Stir-fry for 2 to 3 minutes or to desired doneness. Push meat from center of wok.

Stir sauce; add to center of wok. Cook and stir till thickened and bubbly. Return green onion mixture to wok. Add the spinach and water chestnuts. Stir all ingredients together to coat. Cover and cook about 1 minute more or till heated through.

Serve immediately over hot cooked rice. If desired, sprinkle with slivered orange peel. Makes 4 servings.

Nutrition information per serving: 315 calories, 26 g protein, 35 g carbohydrate, 8 g fat (2 g saturated fat), 54 mg cholesterol, 582 mg sodium.

Beef & Sweet Onion Sandwiches

With sirloin strips instead of ground beef, mustard-sauced sautéed onion, and crisp and colorful vegetables, these beef sandwiches have a definite edge on elegance over hamburgers—and they're just as easy to make.

12 ounces boneless beef sirloin or top round steak, cut 1 inch thick
½ teaspoon coarsely ground black pepper
2 teaspoons cooking oil
1 medium sweet onion (such as Vidalia or Walla Walla), sliced
2 tablespoons Dijon-style mustard
½ of a 7-ounce jar roasted red sweet peppers, drained (about ½ cup)
8 1-inch-thick slices sourdough or marbled rye bread
1½ cups torn prewashed spinach or other salad greens

Trim fat from meat. Sprinkle both sides of meat with black pepper; press in lightly. In a large skillet cook meat in hot oil over medium-high heat about 8 minutes or till slightly pink in center, turning once. Remove from skillet; keep warm.

Add onion to drippings in skillet (add more oil if necessary during cooking). Cook and stir about 5 minutes or till onion is crisp-tender. Stir in mustard; remove from heat.

Meanwhile, cut roasted sweet peppers into ½-inch-wide strips. Toast bread (if desired) and shred spinach or other greens.

Just before serving, thinly slice meat into bite-size strips. To serve, top 4 bread slices with spinach or other greens, meat strips, roasted pepper strips, onion mixture, and remaining bread slices. Makes 4 servings.

Nutrition information per serving: 335 calories, 25 g protein, 30 g carbohydrate, 12 g fat (4 g saturated), 57 mg cholesterol, 553 mg sodium.

Opt for Sweet Onion

Sweet onion is an important part of the flavor of Beef & Sweet Onion Sandwiches (above). Sweet onions, in season April through August, are milder, sweeter, and less pungent than the fall and winter varieties. They have thin, light outer skins and high water and sugar content. Because they are fragile and bruise easily, sweet onions have a short storage life. Vidalia, Walla Walla, and Maui are the most common varieties.

Old-Fashioned Beef Stew

Take the hassle out of dinner tonight by letting this scrumptious stew simmer in your crockery cooker all day.

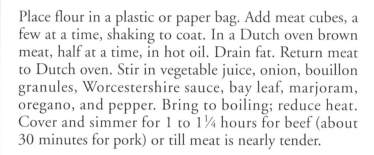

2 tablespoons all-purpose flour
1 pound beef or pork stew meat, cut into ¾-inch cubes
2 tablespoons cooking oil
3½ cups vegetable juice
1 medium onion, cut into thin wedges
2 teaspoons instant beef bouillon granules
2 teaspoons Worcestershire sauce
1 bay leaf
1½ teaspoons snipped fresh marjoram or ½ teaspoon dried marjoram, crushed
1½ teaspoons snipped fresh oregano or ½ teaspoon dried oregano, crushed
¼ teaspoon pepper
2½ cups cubed potatoes
1 cup frozen cut green beans
1 cup frozen whole kernel corn
1 cup sliced carrots

Place flour in a plastic or paper bag. Add meat cubes, a few at a time, shaking to coat. In a Dutch oven brown meat, half at a time, in hot oil. Drain fat. Return meat to Dutch oven. Stir in vegetable juice, onion, bouillon granules, Worcestershire sauce, bay leaf, marjoram, oregano, and pepper. Bring to boiling; reduce heat. Cover and simmer for 1 to 1¼ hours for beef (about 30 minutes for pork) or till meat is nearly tender.

Stir in potatoes, green beans, corn, and carrots. Return to boiling; reduce heat. Cover and simmer about 30 minutes more or till meat and vegetables are tender. Discard bay leaf. Makes 4 servings.

Crockery-Cooker Directions: Prepare and brown meat as above. In a 3½- to 4-quart crockery cooker layer meat, onion, potatoes, green beans, corn, and carrots. Decrease vegetable juice to 2½ cups. Combine the vegetable juice, bouillon granules, Worcestershire, bay leaf, marjoram, oregano, and pepper. Pour over vegetables. Cover and cook on low-heat setting for 10 to 12 hours or till meat and vegetables are tender.

Nutrition information per serving: 458 calories, 30 g protein, 48 g carbohydrate, 16 g fat (6 g saturated), 84 mg cholesterol, 1,261 mg sodium.

Double Salsa Burgers

A fresh tomato salsa flavors the beef mixture and also serves as a colorful topping for these zesty burgers.

1 large tomato, seeded and finely chopped
½ cup finely chopped green sweet pepper
¼ cup finely chopped red onion
2 jalapeño peppers, seeded and finely chopped
1 tablespoon snipped cilantro
1 clove garlic, minced
¼ teaspoon salt
1½ pounds lean ground beef
2 cups shredded lettuce
⅓ cup shredded cheddar cheese
¼ cup dairy sour cream and/or guacamole

For salsa, in a medium bowl combine tomato, green pepper, onion, jalapeño peppers, cilantro, garlic, and salt. Set aside 2 tablespoons of the salsa. Cover and chill the remaining salsa till serving time.

In another medium bowl combine ground beef and the 2 tablespoons salsa; mix well. Shape mixture into six ½-inch-thick oval patties.

Grill patties on an uncovered grill directly over medium coals for 12 to 14 minutes or till meat is no longer pink, turning once.

Arrange shredded lettuce on dinner plates. Top with patties, remaining salsa, and cheddar cheese. Serve with sour cream and/or guacamole. Makes 6 servings.

Nutrition information per serving: 298 calories, 24 g protein, 6 g carbohydrate, 19 g fat (9 g saturated), 87 mg cholesterol, 350 mg sodium.

Handle with Care

Because hot peppers contain oils that can burn your eyes, lips, and skin, protect yourself when working with the peppers by covering one or both hands with plastic bags (or wear plastic gloves). Be sure to wash your hands thoroughly before touching your eyes or face.

Blue Cheese Burgers

Another time, try the easy-to-make blue cheese sauce with grilled steaks.

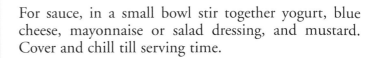

2 tablespoons plain yogurt
2 tablespoons crumbled blue cheese
1 tablespoon mayonnaise or salad dressing
1 teaspoon Dijon-style mustard
1½ pounds lean ground beef
3 green onions, thinly sliced (⅓ cup)
¼ cup chopped green sweet pepper
¼ teaspoon salt
⅛ teaspoon pepper
6 kaiser rolls, split

For sauce, in a small bowl stir together yogurt, blue cheese, mayonnaise or salad dressing, and mustard. Cover and chill till serving time.

Crumble ground beef into a large bowl. Add green onions, green pepper, salt, and pepper; mix well. Shape mixture into six ¾-inch-thick patties.

Grill patties on an uncovered grill directly over medium coals for 14 to 18 minutes or till meat is no longer pink, turning once.

To serve, toast cut sides of kaiser rolls on the grill. Serve patties in toasted rolls. Top patties with sauce. Makes 6 servings.

Nutrition information per serving: 414 calories, 28 g protein, 31 g carbohydrate, 19 g fat (7 g saturated), 74 mg cholesterol, 533 mg sodium.

Stuffed Manicotti with Peppery Cheese Sauce

Walnuts make a surprise appearance in the beefy filling.

12 packaged dried manicotti shells
1 medium onion, chopped (½ cup)
1 clove garlic, minced
3 tablespoons margarine or butter
3 tablespoons all-purpose flour
1½ teaspoons instant chicken bouillon granules
½ teaspoon paprika
¼ to ½ teaspoon ground red pepper
¼ to ½ teaspoon ground black pepper
2¼ cups milk
1 cup shredded process Swiss cheese (4 ounces)
12 ounces lean ground beef or pork
1 cup frozen peas
¾ cup chopped walnuts
2 tablespoons diced pimiento
Sliced green onion (optional)
Diced pimiento (optional)

Cook pasta according to package directions. Drain pasta; rinse with cold water. Drain again.

For sauce, in a medium saucepan cook the chopped onion and garlic in margarine or butter till onion is tender. Stir in flour, bouillon granules, paprika, red pepper, and black pepper. Add milk all at once. Cook and stir till thickened and bubbly. Cook and stir for 1 minute more. Gradually add cheese, stirring till cheese is melted. Remove from heat.

In a large skillet cook ground meat till brown. Drain fat. Stir in peas, walnuts, 2 tablespoons pimiento, and 1 cup of the sauce. Fill each manicotti shell with about ¼ cup of the meat mixture. Arrange filled manicotti in 6 individual au gratin dishes or in 3-quart rectangular baking dish. Pour the remaining sauce over the filled manicotti. Cover with foil.

Bake in a 350° oven about 20 minutes for individual dishes (about 35 minutes for the baking dish) or till heated through. If desired, sprinkle with green onion and additional diced pimiento. Makes 6 servings.

Nutrition information per serving: 515 calories, 26 g protein, 40 g carbohydrate, 28 g fat (8 g saturated), 58 mg cholesterol, 634 mg sodium.

Easy Taco Pizza

This hearty south-of-the border pizza is popular with both kids and adults alike.

Cornmeal Pizza Dough
12 ounces lean ground beef
1 cup chopped onion
1 8-ounce can tomato sauce
1 2¼-ounce can sliced pitted ripe
    olives, drained
1 1¼-ounce envelope taco
    seasoning mix
2 cups shredded cheddar cheese
    (8 ounces)
2 cups shredded lettuce
2 cups chopped tomatoes
2 medium avocados, seeded, peeled,
    and chopped
1 8-ounce carton dairy sour cream
    Chili powder (optional)

Prepare Cornmeal Pizza Dough. Grease two 11- to 13-inch pizza pans or baking sheets. On a lightly floured surface, roll each half of dough into a circle 1 inch larger than pizza pan. Transfer dough to pans. Build up edges slightly. If desired, flute edges. Prick well with a fork. Do not let rise. Bake in a 425° oven for 10 to 12 minutes or till lightly browned.

Meanwhile, in a large skillet cook ground beef and onion till meat is brown and onion is tender. Drain fat. Stir in tomato sauce, olives, and taco seasoning mix. Heat through.

Spread meat mixture over hot crusts. Sprinkle with cheese. Bake about 12 minutes more or till cheese is melted. Top with lettuce, tomatoes, avocados, and sour cream. If desired, sprinkle sour cream with chili powder. Makes 6 servings.

Cornmeal Pizza Dough: In a large bowl combine 1¼ cups *all-purpose flour,* 1 package *active dry yeast,* and ¼ teaspoon *salt.* Add 1 cup *warm water* (120° to 130°) and 2 tablespoons *cooking oil.* Beat with an electric mixer on low speed for 30 seconds. Beat on high speed for 3 minutes. Using a spoon, stir in ¾ cup *yellow cornmeal* and as much of ¾ to 1¼ cups additional *all-purpose flour* as you can. On a lightly floured surface, knead in enough of the remaining flour to make a moderately stiff dough that is smooth and elastic (6 to 8 minutes total). Divide in half. Cover and let rest for 10 minutes.

Nutrition information per serving: 726 calories, 32 g protein, 56 g carbohydrate, 45 g fat (15 g saturated), 90 mg cholesterol, 1,274 mg sodium.

Tamale Pie

Cocoa powder in a main dish pie? Yep! It helps blend the flavors of the other seasonings and gives this entrée a robust background flavor. Although the ingredient list is long, this ground meat pie is a cinch to make.

1¼	cups cold water
½	cup yellow cornmeal
1	teaspoon ground cumin
½	teaspoon paprika
¼	teaspoon salt
¼	teaspoon black pepper
2	teaspoons margarine or butter
1	pound lean ground beef
1	cup chopped onion
1	medium green sweet pepper, chopped (¾ cup)
2	cloves garlic, minced
1	15-ounce can tomato sauce
1	10-ounce package frozen whole kernel corn, thawed
1	tablespoon yellow cornmeal
1	tablespoon chili powder
1	tablespoon ground cumin
2	teaspoons unsweetened cocoa powder
½	teaspoon ground allspice
½	to 1 teaspoon bottled hot pepper sauce
¼	teaspoon black pepper
½	cup shredded sharp cheddar cheese (2 ounces)

In a small saucepan combine water, ½ cup cornmeal, 1 teaspoon cumin, paprika, salt, and ¼ teaspoon black pepper. Bring just to boiling; reduce heat. Stir in the margarine or butter. Cook, uncovered, over low heat for 10 minutes, stirring often. Remove from heat. Spread mixture on waxed paper into an 8-inch square. Chill while preparing meat mixture.

In a large skillet cook ground beef, onion, green pepper, and garlic till meat is brown and onion is tender. Drain fat. Stir in the tomato sauce, corn, 1 tablespoon cornmeal, chili powder, 1 tablespoon cumin, cocoa powder, allspice, hot pepper sauce, and ¼ teaspoon black pepper. Bring to boiling; reduce heat. Simmer, uncovered, for 5 minutes.

Spoon meat mixture into a 2-quart rectangular baking dish. Cut cornmeal mixture into desired shapes, piecing together scraps, if necessary. Place on top of meat mixture.

Bake, uncovered, in a 375° oven about 30 minutes or till bubbly and cornmeal topping is light brown. Remove from oven and immediately sprinkle with cheese. Let stand for 2 to 3 minutes or till cheese is melted. Makes 6 servings.

Nutrition information per serving: 327 calories, 21 g protein, 31 g carbohydrate, 14 g fat (6 g saturated), 57 mg cholesterol, 678 mg sodium.

Chili with Cheesy Cornmeal Dumplings

Fluffy dumplings top this mildly seasoned chili—perfect for a family-style dinner on a wintery day.

12 ounces lean ground beef
1 cup chopped onion
½ cup chopped green sweet pepper
2 cloves garlic, minced
1 15½-ounce can dark red kidney beans, rinsed and drained
1 14½-ounce can tomatoes, cut up
1 8-ounce can tomato sauce
½ cup water
1 tablespoon chili powder
½ teaspoon ground cumin
¼ teaspoon salt
¼ teaspoon black pepper
Cheesy Cornmeal Dumplings

In a large saucepan or Dutch oven cook ground beef, onion, green pepper, and garlic till meat is brown and onion is tender. Drain fat. Stir in beans, undrained tomatoes, tomato sauce, water, chili powder, cumin, salt, and black pepper. Bring to boiling; reduce heat. Simmer, uncovered, for 5 minutes.

Drop Cheesy Cornmeal Dumplings by tablespoonfuls onto simmering chili. Cover and simmer about 20 minutes more or till a wooden toothpick inserted into dumplings comes out clean. Makes 4 servings.

Cheesy Cornmeal Dumplings: In a medium mixing bowl stir together ½ cup *all-purpose flour,* ½ cup shredded *cheddar cheese* (2 ounces), ⅓ cup *yellow cornmeal,* 1 teaspoon *baking powder,* and dash *black pepper.* Combine 1 beaten *egg,* 2 tablespoons *milk,* and 2 tablespoons *cooking oil;* add to flour mixture. Stir with a fork just till combined.

Nutrition information per serving: 528 calories, 35 g protein, 55 g carbohydrate, 22 g fat (8 g saturated), 122 mg cholesterol, 1,108 mg sodium.

Italian Beef Soup

Italian Beef Soup

Keep the ingredients on hand for this easy soup and you'll always be prepared to whip up a hearty supper.

1 pound lean ground beef
2 14½-ounce cans beef broth
3 cups frozen pasta with broccoli, corn, and carrots in garlic seasoned sauce
1 14½-ounce can diced tomatoes
1 5½-ounce can tomato juice or ⅔ cup no-salt-added tomato juice
2 teaspoons dried Italian seasoning, crushed
¼ cup grated Parmesan cheese

In a large saucepan cook ground beef till brown. Drain fat. Stir in beef broth, pasta with vegetables, undrained tomatoes, tomato juice, and Italian seasoning.

Bring to boiling; reduce heat. Simmer, uncovered, about 10 minutes or till vegetables and pasta are tender. Ladle into soup bowls. Sprinkle each serving with Parmesan cheese. Makes 6 servings.

Nutrition information per serving: 258 calories, 20 g protein, 13 g carbohydrate, 14 g fat (6 g saturated), 54 mg cholesterol, 929 mg sodium.

Easy Hamburger-Vegetable Soup

For a simple garnish, sprinkle with bite-size cheese or rich round crackers.

1 pound lean ground beef or pork
½ cup chopped onion
½ cup chopped green sweet pepper
4 cups beef broth
1 cup frozen whole kernel corn
1 7½-ounce can tomatoes, cut up
½ of a 9-ounce package frozen lima beans
½ cup chopped, peeled potato or ½ cup frozen hash brown potatoes
1 medium carrot, cut into julienne strips (½ cup)
1 tablespoon snipped fresh basil or 1 teaspoon dried basil, crushed
1 bay leaf
1 teaspoon Worcestershire sauce
⅛ teaspoon black pepper

In a large saucepan or Dutch oven cook ground meat, onion, and green pepper till meat is brown and onion is tender. Drain fat. Stir in beef broth, corn, undrained tomatoes, lima beans, potato, carrot, basil, bay leaf, Worcestershire sauce, and black pepper.

Bring to boiling; reduce heat. Cover and simmer for 15 to 20 minutes or till vegetables are tender. Discard bay leaf. Makes 4 servings.

Nutrition information per serving: 309 calories, 28 g protein, 25 g carbohydrate, 12 g fat (5 g saturated), 71 mg cholesterol, 958 mg sodium.

Beef and Pasta Salad with Creamy Garlic Dressing

Another time, substitute frozen cut asparagus for the green beans.

1 cup packaged dried corkscrew macaroni or cavatelli

1 cup fresh green beans cut into 2-inch lengths or ½ of a 9-ounce package frozen cut green beans

8 ounces cooked beef, cut into thin strips (1½ cups)

1 medium carrot, shredded (½ cup)

½ cup chopped red onion

½ cup sliced radishes

½ cup mayonnaise or salad dressing

½ cup plain yogurt

2 teaspoons white wine vinegar or vinegar

2 cloves garlic, minced

½ teaspoon dried Italian seasoning, crushed

¼ teaspoon salt

¼ teaspoon dry mustard

1 to 2 tablespoons milk (optional)
Salad savoy leaves (optional)

Cook pasta according to package directions. Drain pasta; rinse with cold water. Drain again. Meanwhile, cook the green beans in a small amount of boiling salted water for 20 to 25 minutes or till crisp-tender. (If using frozen beans, cook for 5 to 10 minutes.) Drain beans; rinse with cold water. Drain again.

In a large bowl combine pasta, green beans, cooked beef, carrot, onion, and radishes. For dressing, in a small mixing bowl stir together mayonnaise or salad dressing, yogurt, vinegar, garlic, Italian seasoning, salt, and dry mustard. Pour dressing over the pasta mixture. Toss to coat. Cover and chill for 4 to 24 hours.

If necessary, stir milk into the pasta mixture before serving. If desired, serve with salad savoy leaves. Makes 4 servings.

Nutrition information per serving: 556 calories, 18 g protein, 25 g carbohydrate, 43 g fat (12 g saturated), 70 mg cholesterol, 360 mg sodium.

Pineapple-Glazed Pork Tenderloin

This sweet and tangy glazed tenderloin, grilled to perfection, is the perfect dish for just about any occasion from an informal family supper to an elegant dinner party.

½ of a 6-ounce can (⅓ cup) frozen
    pineapple juice concentrate
1 tablespoon Dijon-style mustard
1 teaspoon snipped fresh rosemary or
    ¼ teaspoon dried rosemary,
    crushed
1 clove garlic, minced
2 12-ounce pork tenderloins
    Fresh rosemary sprigs (optional)

For sauce, in a small saucepan combine the juice concentrate, mustard, snipped fresh or dried rosemary, and garlic. Cook over medium heat about 5 minutes or till slightly thickened, stirring once. Set aside. Trim fat from meat.

In a covered grill arrange medium-hot coals around a drip pan. Test for medium heat above the pan. Place meat on grill rack over drip pan. Brush with sauce. Cover and grill for 30 to 45 minutes or till slightly pink in center. Brush again with sauce after 15 minutes of grilling. Remove meat from grill and cover with foil. Let stand for 10 minutes before slicing. If desired, garnish with fresh rosemary sprigs. Makes 6 servings.

Nutrition information per serving: 154 calories, 25 g protein, 2 g carbohydrate, 4 g fat (1 g saturated), 81 mg cholesterol, 121 mg sodium.

Pork Medallions with Cherry Sauce

During the autumn months, pork is often prepared with fruit such as prunes or apples. These quick-seared medallions cloaked in a delightful sweet cherry sauce provide a whole new reason—and season—to pair pork with fruit.

1   pound pork tenderloin
    Salt
    Freshly ground pepper
    Nonstick spray coating
¾   cup cranberry juice or apple juice
2   teaspoons spicy brown mustard
1   teaspoon cornstarch
1   cup sweet cherries (such as Rainier
      or Bing), halved and pitted, or
      1 cup frozen unsweetened pitted
      dark sweet cherries, thawed

Trim fat from meat. Cut meat crosswise into 1-inch-thick slices. Place each slice between two pieces of plastic wrap. With the heel of your hand, press each slice into a ½-inch-thick medallion. Remove plastic wrap. Sprinkle meat lightly with salt and pepper.

Spray an unheated large nonstick skillet with nonstick coating. Heat skillet over medium-high heat. Add meat and cook for 4 to 6 minutes or till meat is slightly pink in center, turning once. Remove from skillet; keep warm.

Combine the cranberry or apple juice, mustard, and cornstarch; add to skillet. Cook and stir till thickened and bubbly. Cook and stir for 2 minutes more. Stir cherries into cranberry mixture. Serve over meat. Makes 4 servings.

Nutrition information per serving: 197 calories, 26 g protein, 12 g carbohydrate, 5 g fat (2 g saturated fat), 81 mg cholesterol, 127 mg sodium.

Freezing Cherries

Enjoy Pork Medallions with Cherry Sauce (above) year round by freezing your own supply of summer cherries. Rinse, dry, and pit the cherries. Place cherries in freezer bags or freezer containers, leaving ½-inch headspace. Freeze the cherries for 6 to 12 months. To thaw the cherries, set out at room temperature for 30 minutes.

Pork Tenderloin with Raspberry Sauce

This special occasion dish shows off pork tenderloin with a spicy fruit sauce, fresh star fruit, and berries. Choose a seedless jam for the prettiest appearance.

1   pound pork tenderloin
¼   teaspoon black pepper
2   tablespoons margarine or butter
⅓   cup seedless raspberry or
        strawberry jam
2   tablespoons red wine vinegar
2   teaspoons prepared horseradish
1   clove garlic, minced
¼   teaspoon ground red pepper
        Sliced star fruit (optional)
        Raspberries (optional)

Trim fat from meat. Cut meat crosswise into 1-inch-thick slices. Place each slice between two pieces of plastic wrap. With the heel of your hand, press each slice into a ½-inch-thick medallion. Remove plastic wrap. Sprinkle meat with black pepper.

In a 12-inch skillet melt margarine or butter over medium-high heat. Add meat and cook for 4 to 6 minutes or till slightly pink in center, turning once. Remove from skillet, reserving drippings in skillet. Keep meat warm.

For sauce, stir raspberry or strawberry jam, vinegar, horseradish, garlic, and red pepper into drippings in skillet. Cook and stir till bubbly. Cook about 1 minute more or till slightly thickened. Spoon sauce over meat. If desired, garnish with star fruit and raspberries. Makes 4 servings.

Nutrition information per serving: 282 calories, 25 g protein, 22 g carbohydrate, 10 g fat (3 g saturated fat), 81 mg cholesterol, 157 mg sodium.

Pork Scaloppine with Mustard and Rosemary

To keep the pork warm while you prepare the sauce, place the cooked pork slices on a warm serving platter. Cover with foil and place the platter in a 300° oven.

1	pound pork tenderloin
⅓	cup all-purpose flour
½	teaspoon pepper
¼	teaspoon salt
2	tablespoons margarine or butter
1	tablespoon olive oil or cooking oil
1	cup sliced fresh mushrooms
1	tablespoon snipped fresh rosemary or 1 teaspoon dried rosemary, crushed
2	cloves garlic, minced
¾	cup chicken broth
2	tablespoons Dijon-style mustard
1	teaspoon finely shredded lemon peel
1	tablespoon lemon juice
	Lemon wedges (optional)
	Fresh rosemary sprigs (optional)

Trim fat from meat. Cut meat crosswise into ½-inch-thick slices. Place each slice between two pieces of plastic wrap. With the heel of your hand, press each slice till about ⅛ inch thick. Remove plastic wrap.

In a shallow dish combine flour, pepper, and salt. Coat meat with seasoned flour, shaking off excess.

In a large skillet heat margarine or butter and oil over medium-high heat. Add half of the meat and cook for 3 to 4 minutes or till golden brown on outside and slightly pink in center, turning once. Remove from skillet, reserving drippings in skillet. Keep warm while cooking remaining meat.

Reduce heat to medium. Add mushrooms, snipped fresh or dried rosemary, and garlic to drippings in skillet. Cook and stir just till mushrooms are tender. Add broth, scraping up any browned bits on bottom. Bring to boiling. Boil gently about 5 minutes or till reduced by half. Stir in mustard, lemon peel, and lemon juice. Heat through.

Spoon mushroom mixture over meat. If desired, garnish with lemon wedges and fresh rosemary sprigs. Makes 4 servings.

Nutrition information per serving: 287 calories, 28 g protein, 10 g carbohydrate, 14 g fat (3 g saturated fat), 81 mg cholesterol, 594 mg sodium.

Plum Good Pork Chops

Plum Good Pork Chops

Plum preserves make this glistening glaze simple to make. Try it with grilled chicken or lamb, too.

3 tablespoons plum preserves
1 green onion, thinly sliced
1 tablespoon soy sauce
2 teaspoons lemon juice
⅛ teaspoon curry powder
  Dash ground cinnamon
  Dash ground red pepper
4 pork loin or rib chops, cut
  1¼ inches thick
  (about 2 pounds total)
1 clove garlic, split
  Plum wedges (optional)

For sauce, heat and stir preserves, onion, soy sauce, lemon juice, curry powder, cinnamon, and red pepper over medium heat till bubbly. Trim fat from chops. Rub both sides of chops with cut sides of garlic.

Grill chops on an uncovered grill directly over medium coals for 25 to 30 minutes or till slightly pink in center, turning once. Brush with sauce during the last 10 minutes of grilling. If desired, garnish with plum wedges. Makes 4 servings.

Nutrition information per serving: 224 calories, 20 g protein, 11 g carbohydrate, 11 g fat (4 g saturated fat), 66 mg cholesterol, 283 mg sodium.

Spicy Fruit and Pork Kabobs

Tangy pineapple and cool cantaloupe complement the spicy flavor of this pork on a stick.

1½ pounds lean boneless pork
  2 tablespoons olive oil or cooking oil
  2 tablespoons balsamic vinegar
  1 teaspoon finely shredded orange
    peel
  2 tablespoons orange juice
  1 clove garlic, minced
  ¼ teaspoon salt
  ¼ teaspoon ground cumin
 12 1½-inch cubes fresh pineapple
 12 1½-inch cubes cantaloupe

Trim fat from meat. Cut into 1½-inch cubes. Place in a plastic bag and set bag into a shallow dish. For marinade, combine oil, vinegar, orange peel and juice, garlic, salt, and cumin. Pour over meat; seal bag.

Marinate in the refrigerator for 2 to 4 hours, turning bag once. Drain meat, reserving marinade. Alternately thread meat, pineapple, and cantaloupe onto 6 long metal skewers.

Grill kabobs on an uncovered grill directly over medium coals for 14 to 16 minutes or till meat is slightly pink in center, turning and brushing once with marinade. Makes 6 servings.

Nutrition information per serving: 181 calories, 16 g protein, 6 g carbohydrate, 10 g fat (3 g saturated fat), 51 mg cholesterol, 87 mg sodium.

Szechwan Pork with Peppers

Green and red sweet peppers plus the spicy sweetness of hoisin sauce contrast nicely with the pleasant hotness of the dish. If you want to turn up the heat, add more hot bean sauce.

12 ounces lean boneless pork
 3 tablespoons hoisin sauce
 1 tablespoon hot bean sauce or
       hot bean paste
 1 tablespoon soy sauce
 1 teaspoon sugar
 1 tablespoon cooking oil
 4 cloves garlic, thinly sliced
 1 teaspoon grated gingerroot
 2 medium red sweet peppers, cut
       into 1-inch squares (2 cups)
 2 medium green sweet peppers, cut
       into 1-inch squares (2 cups)
 2 cups hot cooked noodles or rice

Trim fat from meat. Partially freeze meat. Thinly slice across the grain into bite-size strips. Set aside. For sauce, in a small bowl stir together hoisin sauce, bean sauce or paste, soy sauce, and sugar. Set aside.

Add cooking oil to a wok or large skillet. Preheat over medium-high heat (add more oil if necessary during cooking). Stir-fry garlic and gingerroot in hot oil for 15 seconds. Add red and green peppers; stir-fry for 3 to 4 minutes or till crisp-tender. Remove pepper mixture from wok.

Add meat to wok. Stir-fry for 2 to 3 minutes or till slightly pink in center. Add sauce. Cook and stir till bubbly. Return pepper mixture to wok. Stir all ingredients together to coat.

Cook and stir about 1 minute more or till heated through. Serve immediately over hot cooked noodles or rice. Makes 4 servings.

Nutrition information per serving: 292 calories, 18 g protein, 32 g carbohydrate, 10 g fat (3 g saturated fat), 63 mg cholesterol, 1,324 mg sodium.

Great Tasting Gingerroot

Many a stir-fry depends on spicy-sweet gingerroot for its tempting flavor. Look for this knobby root in your supermarket's produce section. Grate or slice as much as you need (peeling isn't necessary). Wrap the remaining root in paper towels and refrigerate it for up to a week. Or, cut up the ginger and place it in a small jar. Fill the jar with dry sherry or wine and refrigerate it, covered, for up to 3 months.

German Grilled Ribs

Apple adds a special flavor to both the ribs and sauerkraut. The sauerkraut heats in a foil packet alongside the ribs.

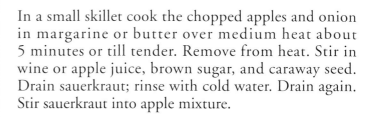

2	medium cooking apples, cored and chopped
1	small onion, chopped (⅓ cup)
1	tablespoon margarine or butter
½	cup dry white wine or apple juice
2	tablespoons brown sugar
1	teaspoon caraway seed
1	16-ounce jar sauerkraut
1½	pounds boneless pork country-style ribs
¼	cup apple butter
	Apple slices (optional)

In a small skillet cook the chopped apples and onion in margarine or butter over medium heat about 5 minutes or till tender. Remove from heat. Stir in wine or apple juice, brown sugar, and caraway seed. Drain sauerkraut; rinse with cold water. Drain again. Stir sauerkraut into apple mixture.

Fold a 36x18-inch piece of heavy foil in half to make an 18-inch square. Place sauerkraut mixture in center of foil. Bring up edges slightly to hold juices. Bring up two opposite edges of foil and seal with double fold. Fold remaining ends to completely enclose sauerkraut mixture, leaving space for steam to build. Trim fat from ribs.

In a covered grill arrange medium-hot coals around a drip pan. Test for medium heat above the pan. Place ribs and foil packet on grill rack over drip pan. Cover and grill for 30 minutes. Brush ribs with some of the apple butter. Cover and grill for 30 to 35 minutes more or till ribs are tender and no longer pink. Brush ribs occasionally with apple butter up to the last 5 minutes of grilling. Partially open foil packet to make a 5-inch opening for last 15 minutes of grilling.

Serve ribs with sauerkraut mixture. If desired, garnish with apple slices. Makes 6 servings.

Nutrition information per serving: 305 calories, 17 g protein, 20 g carbohydrate, 16 g fat (5 g saturated fat), 65 mg cholesterol, 476 mg sodium.

Curried Fruit with Ham Steak

A can of tropical fruit salad jump-starts the tangy, sweet sauce.

1   15¼-ounce can tropical fruit salad in light syrup or one 15-ounce can chunky mixed fruit in light syrup
1   1½-pound fully cooked center-cut ham slice, cut ¾ inch thick
1   small onion, chopped (⅓ cup)
½   to 1 teaspoon curry powder or ⅛ teaspoon ground nutmeg or ginger
1   tablespoon margarine or butter
2   teaspoons cornstarch
¼   cup pineapple juice or orange juice
    Fresh thyme sprigs (optional)

Drain fruit, reserving syrup. Set aside. Trim fat from ham. Place ham on the unheated rack of a broiler pan. Broil 3 to 4 inches from the heat for 12 to 14 minutes or till heated through, turning once.

Meanwhile, for sauce, in a small saucepan cook onion and curry powder, nutmeg, or ginger in margarine or butter over medium heat till onion is tender. Stir in cornstarch. Add pineapple or orange juice and reserved fruit syrup. Cook and stir till thickened and bubbly. Cook and stir for 2 minutes more. Carefully stir in drained fruit. Heat through. Serve warm sauce over ham. If desired, garnish with thyme. Makes 6 servings.

Nutrition information per serving: 232 calories, 24 g protein, 14 g carbohydrate, 8 g fat (2 g saturated fat), 60 mg cholesterol, 1,390 mg sodium.

Sausage and Mostaccioli with Rich Cream Sauce

The rich cream sauce is the perfect foil for sweet and spicy Italian sausage.

 8 ounces packaged dried mostaccioli
   or corkscrew macaroni
12 ounces bulk sweet Italian sausage
   or ground turkey sausage
 2 cups sliced fresh shiitake or button
   mushrooms
 1 small red or green sweet pepper,
   cut into bite-size pieces
 1 medium onion, chopped (½ cup)
 1 clove garlic, minced
1½ cups whipping cream
 2 tablespoons snipped fresh basil or
   ½ teaspoon dried basil, crushed
 ¼ teaspoon black pepper
 ½ cup grated Parmesan cheese
   Fresh basil leaves (optional)

Cook pasta according to package directions. Drain; keep warm. For sauce, in a large skillet cook sausage, mushrooms, sweet pepper, onion, and garlic till sausage is brown. Drain fat.

Stir whipping cream, snipped fresh or dried basil, and black pepper into sausage mixture. Cook over medium-low heat for 5 to 8 minutes or till slightly thickened, stirring occasionally. Remove from heat. Stir in Parmesan cheese.

Arrange the pasta on dinner plates or a large platter. Spoon the sausage mixture over pasta. If desired, garnish with fresh basil leaves. Makes 4 servings.

Nutrition information per serving: 802 calories, 28 g protein, 51 g carbohydrate, 54 g fat (29 g saturated), 181 mg cholesterol, 847 mg sodium.

Pizza Pie

Use a fluted pastry wheel to make decorative cuts in the top crust.

1   15-ounce package (2 crusts) folded
    refrigerated unbaked piecrusts
1   tablespoon cornmeal
8   ounces bulk Italian sausage or
    pork sausage
½   of a 3½-ounce package sliced
    pepperoni
1   4-ounce can mushroom stems and
    pieces, drained
1   8-ounce can pizza sauce
⅛   teaspoon ground red pepper
⅛   teaspoon chili powder
2   cups shredded mozzarella and/or
    cheddar cheese (8 ounces)
1   teaspoon milk or water

Let piecrusts stand at room temperature according to package directions. Lightly grease a 9-inch pie plate. Sprinkle pie plate with cornmeal. Set aside.

Meanwhile, in a large skillet cook sausage till brown. Add pepperoni; heat through. Drain fat. Pat dry with paper towels to remove additional fat. Stir in the mushrooms. Combine pizza sauce, red pepper, and chili powder. Set aside.

Unfold piecrusts. Transfer one of the crusts to prepared pie plate. Sprinkle one-third of the shredded cheese over bottom crust. Pour half of the pizza sauce over cheese. Top with the sausage mixture, another one-third of the shredded cheese, and the remaining pizza sauce. Top with the remaining shredded cheese.

Cut several slits in remaining crust. Place top crust on filling. Trim and flute edge. Brush with milk or water.

Bake in a 425° oven about 30 minutes or till crust is golden brown and pizza is heated through. Let stand for 10 minutes before serving. Cut pizza into wedges. Makes 6 servings.

Nutrition information per serving: 588 calories, 20 g protein, 41 g carbohydrate, 38 g fat (8 g saturated), 70 mg cholesterol, 1,177 mg sodium.